CARYL CHURCHILL

Caryl Churchill has written for the stage, television and radio.
Her stage plays include *Owners* (Royal Court Theatre Upstairs,
1972); *Objections to Sex and Violence* (Royal Court, 1975);
Light Shining in Buckinghamshire (Joint Stock on tour, incl.
Theatre Upstairs, 1976); *Vinegar Tom* (Monstrous Regiment on
tour, incl. Half Moon and ICA, 1976); *Traps* (Theatre Upstairs,
1977), *Cloud Nine* (Joint Stock on tour, incl. Royal Court,
London, 1979, then Theatre de Lys, New York, 1981); *Three
More Sleepless Nights* (Soho Poly and Theatre Upstairs, 1980);
Top Girls (Royal Court, London, then Public Theatre, New York,
1982); *Fen* (Joint Stock on tour, incl. Almeida and Royal Court,
London, then Public Theatre, New York, 1983); *Softcops*
(RSC at the Pit, 1984); *A Mouthful of Birds*, with David Lan
(Joint Stock on tour, incl. Royal Court, 1986); *Serious Money*
(Royal Court and Wyndham's, London, then Public Theatre,
New York, 1987); *Icecream* (Royal Court, London, 1989); *Mad
Forest* (Central School of Speech and Drama, then Royal Court,
London, 1990); *Lives of the Great Poisoners* (with Orlando
Gough and Ian Spink, Second Stride on tour, incl. Riverside
Studios, London, 1991); and *The Skriker* (Royal National
Theatre, London, 1994).

LUCIUS ANNÆUS SENECA

THYESTES

translated and introduced by
CARYL CHURCHILL

NICK HERN BOOKS
London

A Nick Hern Book

Thyestes first published in this translation by Caryl Churchill
in Great Britain in 1995 as a paperback original by Nick Hern
Books Limited, 14 Larden Road, London W3 7ST.

Thyestes translation copyright © 1995 by Caryl Churchill

Front cover image: from Pajou's *L'enfant abrite sous le manteau
de la reine*. Photographer: Paule Muxel Bertrand Desollier.

Typeset by Country Setting, Woodchurch, Kent TN26 3TB
Printed in England by CLE Print Ltd, St Ives, Cambs PE27 3LE

ISBN 1 85459 650 0

A CIP catalogue record for this book is available from the
British Library

THYESTES

Introduction

'Now could I drink hot blood,' says Hamlet,'and do such bitter
business as the day would quake to look on.' He wants to be a
hero in a Seneca play. I didn't know that till I read *Thyestes*.

In the summer of 1992 I went to see Ariane Mnouchkine's
production of the House of Atreus plays, and wondered why
there were no Greek plays about the beginning of the story. But
there had been, James Macdonald told me, though none of them
survived. What did survive was a Latin *Thyestes* by Seneca. I got
the Loeb edition with Latin on one page and English opposite.
At first I was attracted by the Ghost of Tantalus and a Fury, then
by the revenge story, the drought (it was a hot dry summer), the
fears of the world ending, which all felt oddly topical. Then I
started getting interested in the language, in trying to get through
the opaque screen that a translation can't help being to see what
Seneca had actually said. I'd studied Latin at school, and with the
Loeb and a dictionary began to pick my way through a few bits
that interested me.

Loeb's translation was printed in 1912 and though very helpful is
written in a style archaic then: 'Who from the accursed regions
of the dead haleth me forth. . . ' What struck me was how simple
and direct the Latin was. Because it's a language without 'the' or
'a', because it's a language where person and tense are tucked
into the verb (we say 'I will kill', they say 'kill' with endings that
means 'I' and 'in the future'), it uses fewer words than we do and
they're more full of action. In Latin you can say 'black dog kills
white cat, white cat kills black dog, black dog cat white kills, cat
kills white black dog' and it will still be clear that the black dog
killed the white cat because tucked into each word is who's
doing it, who's having it done to them, which colour goes with
which animal, and this means they can achieve subtleties of
emphasis just with word order where we might need a few extra
words.

English is full of Latin words, but for us they're not our most
basic ones, not the ones that mean the thing itself. It's spade *v*

horticultural implement, and it's loving *v* amorous, death *v* mortality, brotherly *v* fraternal. We're lucky to have both and we've gained shades of meaning by having more words to play with. But reading Latin I realised the obvious, that to the Romans Latin words were the only words, the ones that most directly meant the things they wanted to say, not words that were elevated or remote.

So though my vague idea of Seneca, rather confirmed by dipping into translations, had been of a grandiloquent, rhetorical, florid writer, I began to feel he was far blunter, faster and subtler than I'd thought, and I began for my own pleasure to puzzle out what was there. Sometimes I stayed so close to the Latin that I could feel the knobbly foreign constructions just under the English skin, and liked that, though often I made something less literal of it. I put it into verse, counting syllables rather than stresses; often five and six alternating, fives to move faster, or sevens. It forced me to be concise, since something had to be happening in every five syllable line. The choruses have verse patterns done by syllables. I've condensed the choruses a little, but otherwise I feel I've kept close to what Seneca wrote, though my choices of words must be as typical of me and my time as Jasper Heywood's are of him and his time.

Heywood's was the first English translation of *Thyestes*, in 1560. He wrote:

> Thus when my days at length are overpass'd
> And time without all troublous tumult spent,
> An aged man I shall depart at last
> In mean estate to die full well content.
> But grievous is to him the death that, when
> So far abroad the bruit of him is known
> That known he is too much to other men,
> Departeth yet unto himself unknown.

I wrote:

> When my days have passed
> without clatter,
> may I die
> old and ordinary.
>
> Death lies heavily
> on someone who
> known to all
> dies unknown to himself.

Loeb wrote:

> So when my days have passed noiselessly away, lowly may
> I die and full of years. On him does death lie heavily who, but
> too well known to all, dies to himself unknown.

Seneca wrote:

> sic cum transierint mei
> nullo cum strepitu dies
> plebeius moriar senex.
> illi mors gravis incubat
> qui notus nimis omnibus
> ignotus moritur sibi.

Which could be more literally translated as

> so when willhavepassed my
> no with wildconfusednoise days
> oneofthecommonpeople mayIdie old.
> thatone death heavy lieson
> who known toomuch toall
> unknown dies tohimself.

Most of Heywood's translation is written in the rollicking
rhyming alliterative fourteeners that were often used before
blank verse took over:

> What fury fell enforceth me to flee th'unhappy seat,
> That gape and grasp with greedy jaw the fleeing food to eat?

He manages it very skilfully, without getting too trapped by
alliteration. The Penguin collection of Seneca's tragedies gives
excerpts from other Elizabethan translations of Seneca in the
appendix, some far harder to take seriously than Heywood.
I particularly like this, from John Studley's *Medea:*

> O flittring Flockes of grisly ghostes that sit in silent seat
> O ougsome Bugges, O Goblins grym of Hell I you intreat.

Where, I thought, had I heard something like this before? Then I
remembered:

> Thy mantle good,
> What! stain'd with blood?
> Approach ye Furies fell!
> O fates! come, come;
> Cut thread and thrum;
> Quail, crush, conclude and quell.

It is of course 'Pyramus and Thisbe', the play Bottom and his friends are putting on in *A Midsummer Night's Dream*. I hadn't realised before what it was that was being parodied.

Nor had I realised till I read *Thyestes* quite what was meant by Seneca being an influence on Elizabethan theatre, though I'd known it was through Seneca that classical tragedy burst into the sixteenth century – they didn't know the Greek originals. Shakespeare must have had his own reasons from his own time and his own life for writing about horrors, but Seneca showed a way of doing it: ghosts, banished kings, vengeful brothers; drinking blood, asking mountains to fall on you, calling up spirits; night, eclipses, thunderbolts. There are essays or whole books in this, and I'm sure they've been written. And of course it's not all there is to Shakespeare. But the similarities suddenly leapt out at me, and not just the obvious one of *Titus Andronicus*, where the children are served up for dinner.

One of the most specific, following Atreus' thought:

> LEAR. I will have such revenges on you both
> That all the world shall – I will do such things –
> What they are yet I know not – but they shall be
> The terrors of the earth.

And others less close but belonging in the same world that Atreus and Thyestes live in:

> LADY MACBETH.   Come you spirits
> That tend on mortal thoughts, unsex me here,
> And fill me from the crown to the toe top full
> Of direst cruelty. . .
>   . . . Come, thick night,
> And pall thee in the dunnest smoke of hell,
> That my keen knife see not the wound it makes,
> Nor heaven peep through the blanket of the dark
> To cry Hold, hold.

This way of writing and thinking could be used seriously or mocked. When Laertes has jumped into Ophelia's grave –

> Now pile your dust upon the quick and dead
> Till of this flat a mountain you have made
> To o'er top old Pelion. . .

Hamlet sends the whole convention up:

> And if thou prate of mountains, let them throw
> Millions of acres on us till our ground,
> Singeing his pate against the burning zone

Make Ossa like a wart. Nay an thou'lt mouth
I'll rant as well as thou.

I wonder what Shakespeare's attitude is to Lear in the storm.

You sulphurous and thought-executing fires
Vaunt-couriers to oak-cleaving thunderbolts
Singe my white head.

I used to think it was Shakespeare's rhetoric, not Lear's,
Shakespeare's way of writing about Lear's real suffering. But it
seems to me now that the style is deliberately chosen for the
grandiose Lear who demanded speeches of love, and is part of
the self importance he's on the way to losing but hasn't lost yet.

But it's not just words, it's a type of tragic hero that the
Elizabethans found in Seneca, and one of their most popular
plots, revenge plays. It's impossible for us when we see *Hamlet*
to feel the surprise it must have been to its first audiences when
the hero of the revenge play couldn't bring himself to do the
killing. It's as if we'd gone for an evening out and found James
Bond not doing the killing. But even Atreus starts with doubts as
to whether he can manage revenge. Could that have helped
Shakespeare get the idea of putting an Elizabethan melancholic
into a revenge play?

Again and again in his plays Shakespeare worried away at a
problem that worried Seneca – power v the quiet life. Thyestes
comes out of the Forest of Arden back to Corinth. We can't
know if Shakespeare was homesick for Stratford, but we can see
why it was so interesting to Seneca. He was born in Spain in
about 4BC and came with his family to Rome where he held
public office till he was sent into exile in Corsica by the emperor
Claudius for eight years, and there he wrote about Stoicism and
the pleasures of the simple life. He was called back to be tutor to
the boy who soon became the emperor Nero. As Nero's adviser
he may have helped the reign to be relatively peaceful for the
first few years. Seneca was now rich and powerful and deeply
involved in the politics of an increasingly despotic emperor.
When Nero had his mother Agrippina murdered, Seneca
defended him to the Senate, but by 62AD Seneca had had
enough and asked to be allowed to retire. Three years later he
was accused by Nero of plotting against him and told to commit
suicide, which he did with difficulty and courage.

It's not known if Seneca wrote his plays in exile or if they drew
on his experience as Nero's adviser. His whole life was lived in

dangerous times, and Greek stories must have given him a way
of writing about its horrors without being too direct. All his plays
were based on Greek ones – *Phaedra, Trojan Women,
Phoenicians, Oedipus, Agamemnon, Hercules Oetaeus* and
Thyestes. There's a play called *Octavia*, which may have been by
someone copying his style but is extraordinary if it's by Seneca
himself. It has Seneca and Nero as characters and is about Nero
getting rid of his wife. It's extraordinary anyway, a play about
contemporary politics using conventions worked out in rewrites
of Greek tragedies. *Thyestes* was presumably based on Greek
plays, though we don't have any – Sophocles wrote two about
Thyestes, and Euripides another, and there were at least five
other Roman versions which haven't survived.

This is the story of Tantalus and his descendants, which gave so
many writers their plots:

Tantalus was a rich king, a son of Zeus, friends with the gods.
One day when they came to visit he killed his young son Pelops
and served him up for dinner. The gods punished him after his
death by standing him in a stream while a tree dangled fruit near
his mouth – when he tried to eat the tree whisked the fruit away,
when he tried to drink the stream dried up. He was being
tantalised.

Pelops was brought back to life. He wanted to marry a princess,
who would only be given to the man who could beat her father in
a chariot race; losers were put to death. Pelops won by having the
king's axle damaged so that his chariot crashed and he was
killed.

Pelops had two sons, Atreus and Thyestes, who were supposed to
take turns ruling the country and keeping the symbol of power, a
ram with a golden fleece. While Atreus was king, Thyestes
seduced his wife and together they stole the ram. Atreus was
driven into exile and there was civil war. He got into power again
and drove Thyestes out. The play begins here, with Atreus as
king but longing for revenge on Thyestes, who is in exile with
his three sons. By the end Thyestes' sons are dead.

Years later Atreus' sons, Agamemnon and Menelaus go to war
against Troy to get back Helen, Menelaus' wife. To get a
favourable wind, Agamemnon sacrifices his daughter Iphigenia
to the gods. When they come back from Troy Agamemnon is
murdered by his wife Clytemnestra, avenging Iphigenia, and her
lover Aegisthus, another son of Thyestes, avenging his dead

brothers. Urged on by his sister Electra, Orestes, Agamemnon's son, kills Aegisthus and Clytemnestra. He is now in terrible difficulties – the revenge code has broken down since he has only been able to avenge his father by killing his mother, whose murder it would have been his duty to avenge. He is pursued by the Furies until the goddess Athene intervenes to quieten them and bring revenge to an end.

I don't think it's just because I've been translating Thyestes that the news seems full of revenge stories. Seneca could have brought a god on at the end of his play, but he's made a world where gods either don't exist or have left. Or he could have had the chorus back at the end saying the kind of generally uplifting and resigned things they do in Greek plays. But he didn't. The play ends bleakly except for our memory of a chorus who'd hoped for something better.

Caryl Churchill

Characters

GHOST OF TANTALUS, grandfather of Atreus and Thyestes

FURY

ATREUS, king of Argos

MINISTER

THYESTES, Atreus' brother

TANTALUS, Thyestes' son (called after his great-grandfather)
and two other sons who don't speak

MESSENGER

CHORUS

Caryl Churchill's translation of *Thyestes* was first performed at the Royal Court Theatre Upstairs, London, on 7 June 1994 with the following cast:

THE FURY/YOUNG TANTALUS	Sebastian Harcome
CHORUS	Rhys Ifans
MINISTER	James Kennedy
ATREUS	Kevin McMonagle
GHOST OF TANTALUS/THYESTES	Ewan Stewart
THYESTES' TWO YOUNGER SONS *played variously by*	Simeon Hartwig
	Amos Williams
	Debo Adebayo
	Rodney Joseph
	Malachy Rynne
	Jack Fawcett

Directed by James Macdonald
Designed by Jeremy Herbert
Costumes by Jennifer Cook
Lighting by Jon Linstrum
Sound by Paul Arditti

GHOST OF TANTALUS and A FURY

TANTALUS   Who's dragging me
grabbing avidly
up
from the unlucky underworld?
What god's showing where people live?
It's wrong.
Have you found something worse
than burning thirst in
a stream? worse than gaping
hunger? Is it the
slippery stone now for my
shoulders? or the wheel
to tear me apart? or
lying open a
vast cave of guts dug out
to feed dark birds
renewing by night what
you lose by day so
there's always a full meal
for a fresh monster?
What horror am I
being transferred to? O
whoever, harsh judge
of shades who distributes
new tortures, if there's
anything you can add
to these punishments
which even the jailer
of this dire prison
would shudder at and I'm
trembling to think of,
get hold of it. There's a
mob spawned from me who'll
do things so much worse that
I'll look innocent.
If there's any space

available in hell
we'll take it, and while
my lot last the judge of
sin won't sit about.

FURY   Go on, detestable
ghost, drive your gods mad.
Let's have a wickedness
competition, swords
out in every street, no
embarrassment at
being very angry –
blind fury. Then let
rage harden and the long
wrong go into the
grandchildren. No time for
anyone to hate
old crimes because here come
plenty of new ones
and the punishments are
even more wicked.
Whichever brother is
triumphant will lose
the kingdom, the exile
get back in. Fortune
will totter back and forth
between them, power
follow misery and
misery power
and waves of disaster
batter the kingdom.
Driven out for their crimes
when god brings them home
they'll come home to more crimes,
everyone hate them
just as they hate themselves.
Then there'll be nothing
anger thinks forbidden,
brother terrifies
brother, father sons and
sons fathers, children's
deaths are vile and their births
even worse. A wife
destroys her husband,

wars cross the sea to Troy,
the earth is watered with
blood and great leaders
are defeated by lust.
Rape's a joke and love and
laws both fade away.
The sky's not exempt. Why
are the stars shining?
do their flames still owe the
world glory? Let night
be something else. Let day
fall out of the sky.
So stir up your gods, call
hatred, carnage and
funerals, and fill the
whole house with Tantalus.

The columns will be
decorated, the doors
made green with laurel,
fires blaze to celebrate
your arrival home.
Now your crime will happen
all over again.
Why is uncle's hand still? –
Thyestes isn't
crying for his sons yet –
when will it strike? Now
see the cauldron bubble
on the fire, pieces
of chopped up flesh dropped in,
the hearth polluted,
and the great feast prepared.
It's not a new crime
to you so be our guest.
We're giving you a
day of freedom to let
your hunger loose on
this dinner. Sate your fast.
Watch them drink wine mixed
with blood. I've found a feast
you'll run away from –
stop, where are you going?

TANTALUS   Back to the vanishing
            pools and streams and the
            fruit that escapes my lips.
            Let me go back to
            my dark lair. If I'm not
            wretched enough let me
            change streams and stand in the
            river of fire.
            Listen all of you
            punished by fate
            if you're lying trembling
            under an overhang
            fearing the cliff that's
            about to fall on you,
            if you're shuddering at
            the snarling jaws of
            lions or tangling with
            Furies, if you're half
            burnt and fighting off the
            flames, listen to
            Tantalus.
            Believe me. I know.
            Love your punishment.
            When can I escape the
            people who live up here?

FURY   Not till you've churned them up
            to war and the worst
            thing for kings, falling in
            love with weapons. Now,
            shake their wild hearts.

TANTALUS   I should be punished,
            not be a punishment.
            I'm being sent like
            a poisonous gas seeping
            out of the earth or
            a virus scattering
            plague on my people to
            lead my grandchildren to
            horrors. Great father
            of gods and my father
            too even if you're
            ashamed of me, my tongue

may be torn out for
speaking but I won't keep
quiet. I'll warn them.
Don't do this murder.
Don't touch the foulness
the Furies make you crave.
I'll stay here and stop –
What? why attack me
with whips and snakes? what? what's
this clawing hunger
you've thrust deep inside me?
My burnt chest blazes
with thirst, flame flickers
in my scorched belly.
I'm going
wherever
it takes me.

FURY   This this madness rip
through your whole house, like
this like this whirled away
thirsty for blood. Your house
feels you coming and
shudders. What you've done
now is more than enough.
Off to your cave and
stream. The sad land can't bear
you walking on it.
Do you see how water's
driven in away
from the springs, river beds
are empty, how thin
the clouds in the fiery
wind? The trees are all
yellow and bare branches
have lost their fruit, and
where the waves used to roar
now you can hardly
hear them. No more snow on
even the highest
mountain and down below
a terrible drought.
Look, the sun god isn't
sure whether to make

day set off and force it
out in the chariot
to its death.

CHORUS   If any god loves
Argos, its chariot races,
the twin harbours and divided sea,
the snow seen far away on the mountain peaks,
drifted by cold gales,
melted by summer breezes that sail the boats,
if any god is moved
by our clear streams,
turn your gentle spirit.

Stop crime coming back
and grandsons outdoing their
famous grandfather in wickedness.
Why can't they be tired at last and stop?
The little son ran
to his father's kiss and was caught on his sword,
cut up by Tantalus
to make a feast
for his great guests, the gods.

Eternal hunger
followed that meal, eternal
thirst, and that was a good punishment.
Tantalus stands tired out with his throat empty.
Food hangs overhead
quicker to fly away than a flock of birds.
A tree heavy with fruit
plays with his mouth.
He turns his head away.

But the whole orchard
dangles its riches nearer,
ripe apples with languid leaves mock him
till hunger forces him to stretch out his hands –
the fruit's snatched away.
Then thirst starts burning his blood, a cool stream flows
at him then vanishes –
he drinks deep from
the whirling pool, deep dust.

ATREUS and HIS MINISTER

ATREUS   Not brave. Not clever. Not strong.
What I'm really ashamed of
not avenged. After all that.
My brother's tricks. I trusted –
All these empty words. Am I
acting out angry Atreus?
What do I want? the whole world
roaring with armies, both seas
seething with ships, dark fields
and cities shining with flames,
swords glittering as they slash.
I can hear the thunder of
horses. Forests won't hide him
or little stone fortresses
on mountain tops. My people
swarm out of the city and
sing war. If anyone takes
him in and watches over
that head I hate, smash him down
in cataclysmic . . . I
wouldn't care if this palace
fell on me, if it fell on
him too. Do something . . . come on
come on . . . that no one in the
future's going to admire
but no one can stop talking – yes,
I must dare something so bad
so extreme my brother will
wish he'd done it himself. You
don't avenge unless you do
something much worse. And what
could beat what he's done? Is he
ever beaten? Does he stop
at anything when things go
well, and when they go badly
does he stop? I do know the

>   unteachable spirit of
>   the man. It can't be bent, but
>   it can be broken. So. Now.
>   Before he gets organised
>   he must be attacked without
>   warning or while I'm sitting
>   quietly he'll attack. He'll
>   kill or die. There's the crime just
>   there between us waiting for
>   whoever seizes it first.

MINISTER   But what the people will think.

ATREUS   The best thing about being a king,
            people don't just endure
            what you do, they praise it.

MINISTER   They praise from fear. Fear makes enemies.
            Wouldn't you like true praise?

ATREUS   Ordinary people get true praise.
            Only the great get lies.
            Subjects have to want what they don't want.

MINISTER   But if the king wanted what was right,
            no one wouldn't want the same as you.

ATREUS   If a ruler's only allowed what's
            right it's quite a precarious rule.

MINISTER   Where there's no shame or kindness or trust
            I think that's very precarious.

ATREUS   Shame, kindness and trust are qualities
            for private individuals. The
            king can do what he likes.

MINISTER   But you would think it wrong to hurt your
                                              brother.

ATREUS   Whatever's wrong for
            a brother is right
            for him. Because what's
            he ever stopped at?

Wife and kingdom, he
took both. Our ancient
symbol of power
he took by deceit,
by deceit he brought
our family to
confusion. In our
famous flocks there's a
ram whose wool is gold
so all our kings have
gold on their sceptres.
His owner rules. The
future of our house
follows him. He's safe
shut up in a field,
shielded by stone walls,
sacred. The traitor
dared something huge, he
took my wife to help,
he took the ram. This
is what started it.
I've wandered about
a trembling exile
in this country that's
mine. No part of the
family is free
from traps. My wife is
corrupted. The deal
we made to share the
kingdom's smashed. House sick.
Children's blood in doubt.
Nothing certain but
brother enemy.
Why this stupor? Start.
Take hold of your soul.
Think of Tantalus.
That's the kind of thing
my hands are being
asked to do. Tell me
a way to honour
my brother's vile head.

MINISTER   With a sword spit out
his enemy spirit.

ATREUS   You're talking about
                the end of punishment.
                The punishment itself
                is what I want. A
                soft king annihilates.
                In my kingdom death
                is something you beg for.

MINISTER   You feel no respect?

ATREUS   Get out, Respect, if you
                ever lived in this house.
                Cruel throngs of Furies,
                come. Shake your torches.
                My heart doesn't burn with
                enough fury. It
                would help to be filled with
                something more monstrous.

MINISTER   What mad novelty then?

ATREUS   Nothing the limits
                of normal pain can hold.
                There's nothing I won't do
                and nothing's enough.

MINISTER   Sword?

ATREUS   Too small.

MINISTER   What about
                fire?

ATREUS   Still too small.

MINISTER   Then what weapons's any
                use for so much pain?

ATREUS   Thyestes himself.

MINISTER   This is worse than anger.

ATREUS   Yes, I admit it.
                There's an uproar beating

my heart and turning
things over deep inside.
I'm rushed away and
where to I don't know but
I am being rushed
away. The ground bellows,
the clear day thunders,
the whole house creaks as if
the roof were breaking
and the spirits hide their
faces. Let it be
like this. Let it be an
evil you gods are
frightened of.

MINISTER   But what?

ATREUS   I don't know what but
greater than soul and
deeper than custom
and beyond the edge
of what people do
something is swelling
and urging on my
unwilling hands. It's
not that I know what
but it is something
great. All right then. This.
My soul, take it on.
It fits Thyestes,
it fits Atreus,
so we'll both do it
together. This house
long ago saw an
unspeakable feast.
I admit it's a
monstrous sin but it
has been taken on
before. Can my pain
find anything worse?
Stand by me, Procne
and Philomela,
my cause is like yours,
steady my hand. The

greedy father will
happily tear his
children to pieces
and eat his own joints.
It's fine. It's too much.
This is the kind of
punishment I like.
Meanwhile, where is he?
Why is Atreus
harmless for so long?
The whole picture of
slaughter is dancing
in front of my eyes,
bereavement heaped up
in the father's mouth.
My soul, why fall back
in fear? why collapse
before the real thing?
It has to be dared.
Do it. After all
the thing in all this
evil that's really
worst, he'll do himself.

MINISTER   But how will we get him
to step in a trap?
He knows we're enemies.

ATREUS   He couldn't be caught
unless he wanted to
catch us. He's hoping
to get my kingdom. In
this hope he'd run to meet Jove
threatening him with a
thunderbolt, in this hope he'd
dive into the threat of
boiling whirlpools or sail
into straits of treacherous
quicksands, in this hope,
what he thinks the greatest
danger, he'll see his
brother.

MINISTER   Who'll make him trust
                  in peace? who'd he believe?

ATREUS   With desperate hope
                  you believe anything.
                  But my sons can take
                  a message for uncle.
                  Come home, wandering
                  exile, change misery
                  for power and share
                  the rule of Argos. If
                  Thyestes is too
                  hard and spurns my offer
                  his raw sons are tired
                  of pain, easy to catch,
                  they'll be moved by it.
                  His old rage to be king,
                  hunger and hard work,
                  the pain will soften him.

MINISTER   Time will have made his
                  hardship easy.

ATREUS   You're wrong.
                  The sense of pain grows
                  every day. Misery's
                  light. But to go on
                  bearing it gets heavy.

MINISTER   Choose different helpers.

ATREUS   Youth likes to listen to
                  worse lessons than this.

MINISTER   They'll treat their father as
                  you say treat uncle.
                  Wickedness turns on you.

ATREUS   If no one taught them
                  deceit and wickedness
                  power would teach them.
                  Are you frightened they
                  might get bad? They were
                  born to it. You call me

savage and harsh and
think I'm acting cruelly
and with no respect –
don't you think that might be
just what he's doing?

MINISTER   Will your sons know the plot?

ATREUS   You can't trust the young.
They might give us away.
You learn silence from
a lifetime of trouble.

MINISTER   They'll deceive for you
and you'll deceive them?

ATREUS   So they'll be safe from
blame and even from guilt.
Why mix my sons up
in a crime? It's our hate,
let it work through us.
No, you're doing it wrong,
you're shrinking away.
If you spare your own sons
you'll spare his too. Let
Agamemnon know the
plan, Menelaus
know how he helps father.
I can test if I'm
really their father by
how they do this crime.
If they refuse war and
won't wage my hatred,
if they call him uncle,
then he's their father.
All right then, off they go.
But an anxious face
can give a lot away,
great plans betray you
against your will. Better
they don't know how much
of a thing it is. You
hide what we're doing.

MINISTER   I don't need telling.
                It's locked deep in my heart
                by loyalty and
                fear, mainly loyalty.

CHORUS   What fury's driving you
                to keep hurting each other
                and get the throne by crime?
                You're so greedy for power
                you don't know what king means.

                Riches don't make king
                purple robes don't
                nor a crown,
                it's not having golden doors.

                King puts aside fear
                and a cruel heart,
                ambition
                and being loved by the mob,

                doesn't want treasure
                dug in the west
                or the grain
                from Libya's threshing floors.

                He's never shaken
                by thunderbolt
                or gales or
                rough seas or soldiers' lances.

                He's in a safe place,
                looking at things,
                he meets fate
                and doesn't complain at death.

                Though kings gather who
                rule the Red Sea
                and fight those
                who walk on frozen rivers,

                the good mind has a
                kingdom. No need

for horses,
or machines hurling great rocks.

King means fear nothing,
desire nothing.
This kingdom
everyone gives himself.

Let whoever wants
stand powerful
on a peak –
I'd like sweet quiet to fill me.

In an obscure place,
with time for things,
unheard of,
my life will flow through silence.

When my days have passed
without clatter,
may I die
old and ordinary.

Death lies heavily
on someone who
known to all
dies unknown to himself.

THYESTES *and his three sons, the eldest is* TANTALUS.

THYESTES   The roofs of the houses, I've
                longed – the riches of Argos,
                best of all for an exile,
                earth and our own gods (if there
                are in fact gods), there it is,
                the towers the Cyclops built,
                humans can't make such glory,
                the crowd at the racecourse, look,
                I used to be famous for
                winning in father's chariot.

Argos will run to meet me,
crowds of people will run – but
so will Atreus. Go back
and hide in the thick forest,
a life among animals
and just like theirs. This shining
kingdom shouldn't seduce me
with false glitter. Look at the
gift but look at the giver.
Just now when things were all what
everyone calls harsh I was
strong and happy, and now I'm
being rolled round into fear.
My soul stands still and wants to
carry my body backwards,
each step is against my will.

TANTALUS   What is this? he's in a daze,
and looking back and stumbling.

THYESTES   Why are you hanging about
going over and over
something that should be simple?
Do you trust what you know you
can't, brother and power? fear
pain you've already beaten
and tamed, and run away from
hardship you've made good use of?
It's nice now being wretched.
Turn back while you can, get out.

TANTALUS   What's making you turn from our
country now you've seen it? Why
take your love away from such
good things? Your brother throws off
anger, comes back and gives you
half the kingdom, joins up the
dismembered limbs of our house
and restores you to yourself.

THYESTES   You're asking why I'm frightened.
The thing is I don't know.
I can't see anything to
be frightened of but I am

still frightened. I'd like to go
on but my knees give way and
my legs shake so I'm taken
somewhere other than where I'm
trying to get to – kidnapped.
Like a ship using oar and
sail, swept back by a current
that's stronger than oar and sail.

TANTALUS   Wipe out whatever's blocking
your mind and see what prizes
are waiting for you. Father,
you can have the power.

THYESTES   I have the power to die.

TANTALUS   But the highest power is –

THYESTES   Nothing, if you want nothing.

TANTALUS   And you'll leave that to your sons.

THYESTES   The throne doesn't hold two.

TANTALUS   Would anyone want to be
wretched who could be happy?

THYESTES   Listen, that great things make you
happy and harsh ones sad is
lies. When I was high up I
never put panic down, my
own sword on my thigh frightened
me. Oh it's so good to stand
in no one's way, eat dinner
lying on the ground. Killers
don't break into huts, you get
safe food at a plain table,
you drink poison from gold. I
know what I'm talking about.
Bad luck is better than good.
I don't have a house stuck up
on a mountain top to make
people gasp, no high ceilings
gleaming with ivory, no

bodyguards watching me sleep.
I don't fish with a whole fleet
or control the sea with a
massive breakwater. I don't
stuff my stomach with tributes
from tribes, I don't have fields
from the Danube river to
the Caspian sea harvested
for me. I'm not worshipped with
incense and flowers instead
of Jove. I don't have a garden
on my roof or a steam bath.
I don't sleep all day or join
night to night with drink.
I'm not feared. My house is safe
without weapons. And from small things
there comes a great quietness.
You have vast power if you
can manage without power.

TANTALUS   It shouldn't be desired, but
if god gives it, surely it
shouldn't be refused either.
Your brother begs you to rule.

THYESTES   Begs is frightening. There's a
trick in it.

TANTALUS   But brothers can
feel what they used to, and love
can –

THYESTES   Brother love Thyestes?
Oceans will wash the Great Bear,
whirlpools keep still, ripe corn
grow out of the sea, black night
light up the earth. Water and
fire, life and death, wind and sea
are more likely to make peace.

TANTALUS   But what's going to go wrong?

THYESTES   Everything. I don't know what
limit to put to my fear.

He can do as much as he
hates.

TANTALUS   What can he do to you?

THYESTES   I'm not afraid for myself
                any more. It's you who make
                me frightened of Atreus.

TANTALUS   If you're already on guard
                why be afraid of a trick?

THYESTES   It's too late to be on guard
                if you've just stepped in the trap.
                Let it go.
                But get one thing clear:
                I'm following you.
                I'm not leading you.

TANTALUS   God protects good plans.
                Go on. Walk steadily now.

ATREUS   I see him, it's him
                and the children too.
                At last my hate's safe.
                He's coming into
                my hand, Thyestes
                is coming, the whole
                thing. I can hardly
                control my soul, my
                anguish is hardly
                holding the reins. Like
                a hound on a leash
                slowly tracking prey,
                it gets a scent of
                pig far away and
                follows it quietly,
                but when the prey's near
                it struggles and bays

and tears itself free.
When rage smells blood it
doesn't know how to
hide but still it must.
Look at his filthy
hair all over his
face and his foul beard.
Now to keep my word.

How wonderful it is to
see my brother. Give me the
embraces I've longed for.
Whatever anger there's been,
let it go. And from today
nourish the love due to blood
and weed hate out of our hearts.

THYESTES   I could deny the whole thing
if you weren't like this.
But I confess, Atreus,
I confess. I have
done everything you thought.
Your love and duty
have made my case as bad as
possible. A real
villain to be a villain
to such a brother.
I've no advocate but tears.
You're the first person
to see me saying sorry.
These hands which never
touched feet before beseech you,
let our anger go
and let this raging tumour
be cut from our hearts.
As pledge of faith accept these
innocents, brother.

ATREUS   Take your hands off my knees,
come into my arms.
Boys too, arms round my neck,
comforting the old.
Take off your filthy coat
and spare my eyes, take

clothes as good as mine and
be happy sharing
your brother's power. I
get greater glory
by leaving my brother
unharmed and giving
you back father's honour:
having power's luck,
what's good is to give it.

THYESTES   The gods will pay you.
My filthy head refuses
the crown and my unlucky
hand drops the sceptre.
Let me hide in the crowd.

ATREUS   This throne can hold two.

THYESTES   Whatever's yours brother
I'll consider mine.

ATREUS   Who refuses gifts from
fortune when they flow?

THYESTES   Anyone who knows how
easily they ebb.

ATREUS   Can't I have my glory?

THYESTES   You've got your glory
already. Mine's waiting.
To refuse power
is my firm decision.

ATREUS   If you won't accept
your share, I'll give up mine.

THYESTES   I accept. I'll bear
the name of power you're
putting on me but
laws and arms will still serve
you and so will I.

ATREUS
Wear these chains I'm putting
on your head and be
honoured. And I'll make the
sacrifice to the
gods of the victims I've
already chosen.

CHORUS
Will anyone believe this?
Atreus, who can't control his mind,
stood amazed at his brother.
No force is stronger
than what you feel for your family.
Strangers' quarrels last
but if you're joined by love you're joined forever.

When both sides have good cause
to make them angry,
and Mars keeps the swords striking
in his thirst for blood,
love forces you into peace.

What god's made this sudden quiet?
Civil war was wrecking the city.
Pale mothers clung to their sons.
We mended the walls
and mouldy towers, and barred the gates.
Pale watchmen stared at
anxious night: worse than war is the fear of war.

Now it's swords that have fallen,
the trumpets are still,
clashing clarions are silent.
Deep peace has come back
to the delighted city.

When a north wind churns the waves
sailors are afraid to put to sea
as Charybdis gulps it in
and vomits it out,

and Cyclops is afraid Etna's fire
   that roars in his forge
may be put out by a great surge of water.

  But when the wind drops the sea's
    gentle as a pool.
  Ships were afraid but now
    small boats are playing.
  There's time to count the fishes.

  No luck lasts, pain and delight
take it in turn – delight's turn's shorter.
  Time flings you from low to high.
    If you wear a crown
  and tribes lay down their arms when you nod,
    soon everything shifts
and you fear how things move and the tricks
                    of time.

  Power over life and death –
    don't be proud of it.
  Whatever they fear from you,
    you'll be threatened with.
All power is under a greater power.

  You can be great at sunrise,
    ruined by sunset.
  Don't trust good times too much or
    despair in bad times.
  The old women mix things up
    and spin every fate.
  No one has gods so friendly
he can promise himself tomorrow.
  God turns our quick things over
    in a fast whirlwind.

MESSENGER   A whirlwind to fly me
            headlong through the air
            and roll me in a black cloud
            so the horror's ripped out of my eyes.
            O house even Tantalus
            would be ashamed of.

CHORUS   What news do you bring?

MESSENGER   So where are we now? Argos?
            Sparta, whose brothers
            love each other? Corinth with
            twin seas? no maybe
            on the wild frozen Danube,
            with Caspian tribes
            under eternal snow or
            with the Scythians
            who just wander anywhere?
            what is this place that's
            in on this unspeakable...

CHORUS   Speak and open up
            whatever it is.

MESSENGER   If my soul would keep still.
            If my rigid body
            would let go of my limbs.
            The violence sticks to my eyes.
            Take me far away,
            senseless tempests, take me where
            day is taken when it's snatched.

CHORUS   You're keeping my soul
            in suspense that's worse.
            Say why you shudder
            and say who did it.
            Not who but which one.
            Just say it quickly.

MESSENGER   On top of the citadel
            part of the palace faces
            the south winds. It's high as a
            mountain and presses on the
            city, the people kick at

kings – it's got them where it can
strike. There's a huge glowing hall
that can hold a crowd, columns
brightly painted, golden beams,
but behind what everyone
knows about and can visit
the rich house divides into
more and more spaces – furthest
in, a secret place, a deep
hollow with old woods, the most
inward bit of the kingdom.
No cheery fruit trees here, just
yew and cypress and groves of
black ilex shifting about
and above them one tall oak
sticks up and masters the wood.
From here kings start their new reigns,
here they ask for help when it
all goes wrong. They stick up their
gifts here – noisy war trumpets
and broken chariots, wheels whose
axles were tampered with so
they'd win – all the things they've done,
Pelops' turban, all their
loot, a decorated shirt,
triumph over barbarians.
In the shadows there's a
sad spring that seeps through
black mud, like the ugly
water of Styx that
heaven swears by. They say
gods who deal with death
groan here in the blind night,
chains clank and ghosts howl.
Whatever you're frightened
to hear of, you see.
Wandering about, out of
their graves, turbulent
gangs who lived long ago,
and monstrosities
worse than you've ever seen
jump out. Even worse
the woods glitter with flames,
trees blaze without fire.

Something keeps bellowing
and the house is struck
with terror at huge shapes.
Day doesn't calm fear,
the grove is its own night,
at noon you still feel
this horror of spirits.
Seek an oracle,
with a huge din the fates
are loosed from the shrine,
the cave bellows a voice
as god is released.

When Atreus arrived
in a rage dragging
his brother's children, the
altars were decorated . . .
who can describe it
as it really was?
He ties the princes' hands
behind their backs, ties purple
ribbon on their sad heads;
no shortage of incense
or holy wine or salty
flour to sprinkle on the
sacrifice. The ritual's kept
in case evil's not done right.

CHORUS   Who takes hold of the knife?

MESSENGER   He's the priest himself.
He sings the death song,
prays violently,
stands at the altar,
the consecrated
sacrifices he
handles himself and
arranges them and
takes hold of the knife.
He pays attention,
nothing sacred's lost.
The grove's trembling, the
whole palace is shaken
from below, and it

totters, unsure where to put
its weight, and seems to move
up and down in waves.
From the left of the sky
a star runs dragging
a dark trail. The wine turns
bloody in the fire,
his crown keeps falling off,
ivory statues weep.
Everyone's moved by these
monstrous portents but
Atreus stands unmoved
and frightens the gods
who thought they'd frighten him.
And now he's standing
at the altar with a
savage sideways look.
Like a tiger in the
jungle between two
bulls, greedy but not sure
which to bite, turning
her jaws to this one then
looking back, keeping
her hunger waiting, he
eyes the victims and
wonders which to kill first.
It doesn't matter
but he enjoys putting
murder in order.

CHORUS   So which does he attack?

MESSENGER   First place (no lack of
            respect) dedicated
            to grandfather, so
            Tantalus goes first.

CHORUS   How did the boy look,
            how did he face his death?

MESSENGER   He looked unconcerned, there's
            no point pleading, then
            the savage buried the
            knife in the wound and

pressed it in so deep
the hand reached the throat.
When he pulled the blade out
the corpse still stood there
not sure which way to fall,
then fell on uncle.
He dragged Plisthenes
to the altar and
put him by his brother.
He struck his neck and
cut through the nape so the
body crashed forward
and the head rolled away
with a querulous
sort of gasp or growl.

CHORUS   When he'd carried out two
killings what did he do?
Did he spare the boy
or heap crime on crime?

MESSENGER   You know what a lion's
like killing cattle,
its jaws are wet with blood
and its hunger's gone
but it can't let go of
its anger, it keeps
running at the bulls and
threatening the calves, but
it's tired and lethargic –
that's how Atreus was,
swollen with anger,
holding the bloodstained knife,
forgetting who he's
angry with, he drove right
through the body with
his murdering hand. The
knife's gone through the chest,
it's sticking out the back,
the boy falls, he'd have
died from either wound.

CHORUS   Crime of a savage.

MESSENGER   Does it make you shudder?
             If the evil stopped here
             we'd think it was good.

CHORUS   Does nature allow
             anything more cruel?

MESSENGER   You think this is the
             extreme limit of crime?
             It's the first step.

CHORUS   What more could he do?
             Maybe he threw the
             bodies to wild beasts
             and refused them fire.

MESSENGER   I wish he had. I
             don't want earth covering
             them or fire burning.
             He can give them to birds
             or drag them off as
             food for wild animals.
             After what happened
             you'd pray for things that are
             usually torture.
             I wish their father could
             see them unburied.
             Unbelievable crime,
             people will say it
             could never have happened.
             Vitals tremble, torn
             from living breasts and
             veins breathe and hearts still leap.
             But he handles them
             and tells fortunes from the
             veins on the entrails.
             When the animals are
             satisfactory, he's
             free for his brother's feast.
             He cuts the body in
             chunks, severs shoulders
             and difficult muscles
             of the upper arms,
             lays open the hard joints

and cuts through the bones.
He keeps their faces
and the hands they gave him.
Offal stuck on spits
dripping over slow fires,
or bubbling in water.
Fire jumps over the feast
and two or three times
it's carried back to the
hearth and forced to burn.
The liver's hissing – it's
hard to say if fire
or flesh protested most.
The fire goes out in
pitch black smoke, and the smoke,
a thick fog, doesn't
go straight up to the sky,
it settles all around
in an ugly cloud.

Phoebus, god of the sun,
who suffers so much,
even though you've fled back
and plunged the broken
day out of the sky, still
you've set too late. The
father's tearing up his
sons and chewing his
own flesh, he looks splendid
his hair wet with oil
heavy with wine, sometimes
his throat closes and
holds back the food.
In all this evil, one
good thing, Thyestes,
you don't know the evil,
but that'll pass too.
Even though the sun god
turned his chariot back,
and sent night from the east
at a strange time to
bury the foul horror
in a new darkness, still
it must be seen. All
evils get laid open.

CHORUS

Sun, where have you gone?
how could you get lost
half way through the sky?
 The evening star's not here yet,
the chariot hasn't turned in the west
    and freed the horses,
the ploughman whose oxen still aren't tired
  can't believe it's suppertime.

The way things take turns
in the world has stopped.
There'll be no setting
 any more and no rising.
Dawn usually gives the god the reins,
    she doesn't know how
to sponge down the tired sweating horses
  and plunge them into the sea.

Whatever this is
I hope it is night.
I'm struck with terror
 in case it's all collapsing,
shapeless chaos crushing gods and men.
    No winter, no spring,
no moon racing her brother, planets
  piled together in a pit.

The zodiac's falling.
The ram's in the sea,
 the bull's bright horns drag
 twins and crab, burning lion
brings back the virgin, the scales pull down
    the sharp scorpion,
the archer's bow's broken, the cold goat
  breaks the urn, there go the fish.

Have we been chosen
out of everyone
somehow deserving
 to have the world smash up and
fall on us? or have the last days come
    in our lifetime? It's
a hard fate, whether we've lost the sun
  or driven it away.

Let's stop lamenting.
Let's not be frightened.
You'd have to be really
    greedy for life
if you didn't want to die when the whole world's
    dying with you.

ATREUS

I'm striding as high as the
stars, I'm above everyone,
my head's touching heaven. Now
I've the kingdom's glory and
father's throne. I'm letting the
gods go, I've got all my prayers.
It's fine, it's too much, it's
enough even for me.
But why should it be enough?
I'll keep going and cram him
full of his sons' death. Day's left
so shame won't get in my way.
On, while the sky's empty. I
do wish I could stop the gods
escaping and drag them all
to see my revenge. But no,
it's enough if the father
sees it. Without daylight I'll
scatter the darkness for you.
You've been lying there too long
having a nice feast, enough
food, enough wine, Thyestes
needs to be sober for this.

Open the temple doors.

I look forward to seeing
what colour he'll go when he
sees his children's heads, what words
his first pain will break out in,
how his body will stiffen.
This is what I've worked for. I

don't want to see him wretched,
just when he's getting wretched.

The hall's gleaming with torches.
He's lying on purple and
gold, heavy head on his hand.
He belches. O wonderful
me, I'm a god, I'm king of
kings. I've done more than my prayers.
He's had enough to eat. He's
drinking unmixed wine from the
silver cup – don't hold back on
the drink. There's still the blood, the
colour of wine will hide it.
With this this cup the meal ends.
I want the father to drink
his children's blood – he would have
drunk mine. Look, he's singing now,
and can't control what he thinks.

THYESTES
Heart dulled so long
with terrible wrong
put away care
get rid of despair
no more the shame
of losing your name
It's more important where you
fall from than where you fall to.
It really is great
if you fall from a height
to stand on the plain
and walk on again.
It really is great
to bear all the weight –
But the bad times are over
so we'll forget all that.
The good are happy again, let good times roll,
and send the old Thyestes out of my soul.

A weakness of the
wretched, you never
believe you're happy.
Good luck comes back but
it's still hard for the

damaged to smile. Why
do you call me back
and stop me celebrating?
why make me cry, pain
surging up out of nowhere?
why not let me put
flowers in my hair?
It won't it won't let me. The
roses have fallen
off my head, my hair's
sleek with oil but it's
standing on end with
horror, I can't help
tears on my face and
groans get in my words.
Grief loves the tears it's used to
and the wretched get a
terrible desire to cry.
It's nice complaining,
it's nice tearing your
clothes, it's nice howling.
My mind's warning me
something bad's coming.
With no wind, smooth waters swell,
and that means a storm.
But what could it be?
Are you crazy? Trust
your trusting brother.
By now, whatever it is,
it's nothing or it's too late.
I don't want to be
unhappy. But inside
I've aimless terror
wandering about, I
burst into tears
and there's no reason.
Is it grief or fear?
Or does great joy make you cry?

ATREUS   We'll always celebrate this
day with a feast, brother,
it makes my sceptre strong and
binds us in certain peace.

THYESTES   Enough food and even
            enough wine. The one thing
            that could add to my pleasure –
            share my joy with my children.

ATREUS   Think of your sons as here
            held tight by their father.
            Here they are and always
            shall be. No one's going
            to take your children
            away from you. I'll
            bring you the faces
            you're longing to see
            and give father his
            fill of family.
            You'll have enough of them.
            They're mixing, taking
            part in the feast, a
            young dinner, good fun,
            but I'll get them. Take this cup,
            it's an old family wine.

THYESTES   I take this gift from my
            brother, we'll pour wines to our
            father's gods, then drain them –
            but what's this? my hands
            won't do it, weight's growing
            making my right hand
            heavy; when I lift the
            wine it gets away
            from my lips, it's spilling
            round my jaw cheating
            my mouth, and the table's
            jumping up from the
            floor. The lights hardly shine.
            And now the heavy
            sky's deserted, between
            day and night, it's stunned.
            Now what? more and more its
            arch is shaken, it's
            tottering, a thicker
            fog's gathering with
            dense shadows and night is
            added to night. The

stars have all run away.
Whatever it is
I pray it spares my
brother and children
and the whole storm breaks
on this vile head. Now
give me back my sons.

ATREUS

I'll give you them and
the day shall never come
to take them away.

THYESTES

What's this uproar churning
my stomach? what's this
shaking inside? I can't
bear the load I feel
and my chest groans with a
groaning that's not mine.
Children, come here, your
unhappy father's
calling you, come here. This
pain will go when I
see your faces. Do I
hear their voices? where?

ATREUS

Open your arms, father,
they're coming now.
Do you by any chance
recognise your sons?

ATREUS *shows* THYESTES *their heads.*

THYESTES

I recognise my
brother. Earth how can you
bear all this evil?
Aren't you bursting open
and plunging to the
underworld and snatching
kingdom and king down
a vast road to chaos?
smashing the palace
and turning Mycenae
upside down? By now
both of us should be with

Tantalus. And there
and there break it open,
if there's anything
lower than hell and our
grandfather make a
huge chasm and hide us,
buried under the
river. Guilty souls can
wander over our
heads and the fiery flood
pour lava over
our exile. But earth is
unmoved. Heavy and
still. The gods have left.

ATREUS   You should be happy
to see them, you kept on
asking for them. Your
brother's not stopping you.
Enjoy, kiss, embrace.

THYESTES   Was our treaty this?
Is this your friendship,
is this a brother's love?
Let our hate go? I'm
not asking to be a
father with his sons
back unharmed. Just what
can be given with
crime and hate still whole,
I ask as a brother.
Let me bury them.
Give what you'll see burnt.
I'm not asking for
what I'll keep, just
what I'll lose.

ATREUS   Whatever's left of
your sons, you've got it.
Whatever's not left,
you've got that too.

THYESTES   Are they lying out as
food for fierce birds or

thrown to dogs or to
feed wild animals?

ATREUS   You've eaten your sons yourself.

THYESTES   This is what shamed the
gods and drove day back.
What voice can I give
to my misery? what
lament? what words will
be enough for me?
I can make out the
heads that were cut off,
hands ripped away, feet
wrenched from broken legs –
what even greedy
father couldn't eat.
Their flesh is heaving
inside me and the
evil shut in is struggling
with no way out and
trying to escape.
Your sword, brother, the
one with my blood on.
I'll make the children
a way out with steel.
You won't? I'll break my
chest by beating it.
No, hold back your hand,
leave their souls in peace.
Whoever saw such
evil? Do wild tribes
on the rocks of the
Caucasus do this?
Was Procrustes worse,
terrorising . . .? Look
I'm crushing my sons
and they're crushing me.
Is there any
limit to crime?

ATREUS   Crime should have a limit
when you commit a crime,
not when you avenge it.

Even this is too
little for me. Hot blood
straight out of the wound
into your mouth while they
were still alive, yes,
my anger was cheated
because I hurried.
I attacked them with a
sword, brought them down at
the altar, fed the fire
with their blood, hacked the
bodies and tore them to
small chunks that I plunged
into boiling water
or grilled on slow fires.
I cut still living flesh,
I fixed the offal
on thin spits and watched it
hissing and fed the
flames with my own hands. And
all this the father
could have done much better.
This pain is no use.
He tore his sons apart
but he didn't know
and they didn't know.

THYESTES   Shut in by shifting shores,
hear me, seas, and you hear this
crime, gods, wherever you've run;
hear, underworld, hear, lands, and
night, heavy with hell's black clouds,
have time for my cries, (I've been
left to you, only you see my
misery, you who've been left
by the stars) I won't pray for
anything wicked, I can't
ask anything for myself,
what could there be for me now?
It's you I'm praying for.
Whoever's in charge of the
sky and is lord of the air,
wrap the whole earth in rough clouds,
from every side at once send

wars of winds, and thunder. And
not with the hand that seeks out
ordinary houses that
don't deserve any harm, but
the one by which the massive
mountains fell and the Giants
who stood as tall as mountains –
send those weapons. Twist your fires.
Make up for the lost day, launch
flames, give us lightning instead
of the light snatched from the sky.
Don't waste time on a judgment –
call both our causes bad. Or
anyway let mine be bad.
Aim at me, send a flaming
brand forked like an arrow through
this body. To bury my
sons as a father should and
give them to the last fire, I
must be cremated.
But if nothing moves the gods
and no spirit punishes
the wicked, then I'd like the
night to last forever and
cover the vast crime
with endless dark. I've nothing
to complain about if the
sun stays gone.

ATREUS   Now I can praise my hands.
            Now I've really won.
            I would have wasted my
            wickedness if you
            didn't suffer like this.
            Now I believe my
            children are really mine,
            now I get back my
            faith in my marriage.

THYESTES   How did my children deserve . . . ?

ATREUS   Because they were yours.

THYESTES   Sons killed for the father –

ATREUS   Yes, and what makes me happy
              mine are mine and yours are yours.

THYESTES   Where were the gods who
              protect the innocent?

ATREUS   Where were the marriage gods?

THYESTES   But who'd try to balance
              a crime with a crime?

ATREUS   I know what it is
              you're complaining about.
              You're suffering because
              I snatched the crime away,
              you're not grieving at
              gorging forbidden food
              but because you weren't
              the one to prepare it.
              You'd have liked to set up
              just this sort of feast
              for your brother who
              wouldn't have known what
              was going on and
              get their mother to
              help you attack my
              children and throw them
              down to the same death.
              Just one thing stopped you –
              you thought they were yours.

THYESTES   Avenging gods will come.
              I leave you to them
              for punishment.

ATREUS   For punishment
              I leave you to your children.